BUDDHISM

How To Truly Experience Mindfulness And Happiness Every Day Through Buddhism

By accepting to read this book, you understand that there is a risk of injury associated with applying the information that contains this book, either mental or physical. You hereby assume full responsibility for any and all injuries, losses and damages. The information contained in this book is for general information purposes only.

The information is provided by our company and while we endeavor to keep the information up to date and correct, we make no representations or warranties of any kind, express or implied, about the completeness, accuracy, reliability, suitability or availability with respect to the information contained on the book for any purpose. Any reliance you place on such information is therefore strictly at your own risk. We remind you that you should always consult your physician or other healthcare provider before changing your diet or starting an exercise program. You should always consult a therapist before starting mental exercises, or any kind of program related to self-help.

This document is geared towards providing exact and reliable information in regards to the topic and issue covered. The publication is sold with the idea that the publisher is not required to render accounting, officially permitted, or otherwise, qualified services. If advice is necessary, legal or professional, a practiced individual in the profession should be ordered.

From a Declaration of Principles which was accepted and approved equally by a Committee of the American Bar Association and a Committee of Publishers and Associations.

The information provided herein is stated to be truthful and consistent, in that any liability, in terms of inattention or otherwise, by any usage or abuse of any policies, processes, or directions contained within is the solitary and utter responsibility of the recipient reader. Under no circumstances will any legal responsibility or blame be held against the publisher for any reparation, damages, or monetary loss due to the information herein, either directly or indirectly.

Respective authors own all copyrights not held by the publisher.

The information herein is offered for informational purposes solely, and is universal as so. The presentation of the information is without contract or any type of guarantee assurance.

The trademarks that are used are without any consent, and the publication of the trademark is without permission or backing by the trademark owner. All trademarks and brands within this book are for clarifying purposes only and are the owned by the owners themselves, not affiliated with this document.

CONTENTS

INTRODUCTION

WHAT DO YOU want for your life? If you could have anything you wanted, what would that be? If this question was posed to fifty people, you would probably get a variety of answers. But regardless of what responses they give, that response would have an underlying desire; the desire to be happy. This is why we want relationships, money, a new job, good health, security, love, to live in a better neighborhood, and so on...we believe that which we desire will bring us happiness. There is a Buddhist parable that goes something like this:

> *There is a poor man who lives his life out wandering the country, begging strangers for food and coins. One day, the poor man comes across a friend who he has not seen for many years. The friend feels sorry for the poor man and invites him to his home to have a decent meal and a bed to sleep in. Unlike the poor man, the friend is very rich and lives a life of luxury.*
>
> *During the night, the friend sneaks into the room*

1

where the poor man is sleeping and sews a precious jewel within the lining of the poor man's robe. The next day, the poor man thanks the friend for his hospitality and continues on his wandering through the countryside.

Years go by before the friend and the poor man encounter each other again. The friend sees that the poor man has continued to live out his life begging and struggling. The friend looks at the poor man in a disappointing manner and informs the poor man of the precious jewel within the lining of his robe; that he'd had the wealth to buy anything he wanted, yet he continued to live a life of hardship and lack.

Most of humanity is like the poor man, in that our lives become an endless pursuit for the people, objects, or situations that we believe will make us happy. Our attention has an outward focus, preventing us from coming to the realization that an inexhaustible treasure of wisdom, power, equanimity, courage, and faith lies within us. For within every being, there lies the precious jewel of enlightenment.

Until we come to this realization, our lives become an endless cycle of desires and attempts to satisfy them. There is nothing wrong with having desires or working to fulfill them. This is both a necessary and an enjoyable part of life. The problem arises when we allow the conditions of our lives to shape our sense of happiness.

We are blind to the precious jewel that lies within us. It is from this inability to recognize this jewel that all of our problems arise, without exception. When you can recognize this jewel within, you will achieve what all of humanity is looking for; true happiness.

This is the purpose of Buddhism, to discover this jewel. I welcome you to this most special journey; a journey of the most profound discovery.

CHAPTER 1
A BRIEF HISTORY OF BUDDHISM

SIDDHARTHA GAUTAMA WAS born in India in the year 623 B.C. Born into royalty, Siddhartha was sheltered from the social ills of society as he never left his family's palace, per the request of his father. His father wanted Siddhartha to inherit the throne; however, that all changed when the prince turned 29 years old.

Siddhartha began to leave the palace as he wanted to learn what the outside world was like. Outside the protection of the palace walls, Siddhartha witnessed the realities of life. He saw the suffering brought about by aging, by disease, by poverty, and by death. From that point on, Siddhartha made it his life's mission to find a way to ease the suffering of people.

He left the palace, to the dismay of his parents and wife, and spent the next 10 years following the teachings of the spiritual teachers and ascetics of his time. He dedicated himself to the numerous practices that he became a student of, often enduring severe deprivation. He subjected his body to the absolute minimal amount of food and drink needed to survive; he denied himself shelter, exposed his body to the harshness of the elements, and he subjected his body to unnatural positions for prolonged periods of time. He did all of this to become enlightened, to understand how to overcome suffering.

Despite his mastering the teachings and practices he was taught, he was unable to find what he was looking for. Siddhartha left the ascetic lifestyle, nourished himself back to health, and started to meditate. He sat under the Bodhi tree and made the determination that he would not move until he became enlightened.

During his meditation, he experienced numerous visions. Thoughts and desires that were presented to him by his mind, all of them competing to distract his attention from his meditation; however, Siddhartha persisted in his meditation and eventually did reach enlightenment. He became the Buddha; a word meaning 'awake.'

The Buddha spent the rest of his life traveling throughout India where he spread his teachings to all that would listen. The Buddha teachings were transmitted orally, nothing was written. When he died, his disciples transcribed his teachings in the form of sutras, which then spread to China, Japan, Asia, and eventually the West. It is from this transmission that his teachings became a world religion. As Buddhism spread it developed different lineages. The main lineages are Theravada, Mahayana,

Tibetan, and Japanese.

Theravada is one of the oldest schools of Buddhism and is both monastic and orthodox in its teachings. Its teachings seek to understand human nature through the transformation of consciousness. This is done through meditation, ethical conduct, and the development of insight and wisdom.

Mahayana Buddhism is less monastic than Theravada, has more rituals, and its teachings are more fluid, adapting to differences in cultures and the changing of times. It strives for the enlightenment of all sentient beings and teaches that the pursuit for enlightenment must involve the working for the happiness of others; the enlightenment of the individual is dependent on working for the enlightenment of others.

Tibetan Buddhism is one of the more recent lineages of Buddhist schools and has spread widely from its origins in Tibet and is well known in the West. This is the Buddhist school that the Dali Lama belongs to. Its rituals include offerings of food, mediation, prayer, and chanting.

Japanese Buddhism originated from China and then branched out into different schools. Some of the more commonly known schools are Zen Buddhism and Nichiren Buddhism. Zen Buddhism has few if any rituals; rather, practitioners use meditation to break through the barriers of the mind that prevent the experiencing of expanded awareness, known as Satori. Nichiren Buddhism is commonly practiced in the west and has organizations in most parts of the world. Practitioners of this Buddhism chant to a mandala, known as the Dai Gohonzon, which symbolizes the enlightened nature that exists within the life of all sentient beings.

CHAPTER 2
WHY PRACTICE BUDDHISM...IN A NUTSHELL

IMAGINE YOU ARE in a theater watching a movie. This movie is full of drama, suspense, action, and comedy. You are riveted to the movie screen as you lose awareness to everything that is happening around you; you are totally absorbed in the movie. With each passing scene, you experience a shift in emotion. During the course of the movie, you experience anticipation, concern, fear, anger, happiness, sadness, laughter, and suspense. Your state of being is as though it is on a roller coaster ride as each scene elicits a change in emotion or feeling.

Now imagine this situation, you are watching the same movie, and you are enjoying the range of thoughts, feelings, and emotions that come from experiencing the movie; however, you are also fully aware of what is happening around you in the theater; you are aware that it is just a movie and do not get caught up in it. The movie may elicit a wide range of emotions from you; yet, a sense of peace or calm remains with you. You enjoy your movie experience fully, while never forgetting it is just a movie.

These two scenarios are a metaphor for life. You are the one that is watching the movie, while the movie is your mind. The first scenario represents the lives of most of us. We are totally absorbed in our thoughts, memories, beliefs, and perceptions. This creates our sense of identity and our experience of life.

Without exception, all of our problems and sufferings, individually or collectively, arise because we are absorbed in our mind; we are absorbed in the movie.

Practicing Buddhism is like the second scenario. You fully enjoy the movie but you do not get caught up in it. You know it is just a movie; you understand that the truth of life is so much more than the movie can ever depict.

By practicing Buddhism, our sense of self becomes like a sail boat as it effortlessly moves through the calm waters of the mind. When we do not develop this understanding, our sense of self constantly changes in response to the situation at hand.

We can see this more clearly by using an imaginary scenario. Rob wakes up Monday morning at 7:00 a.m. and goes for his morning jog. As he is running, he witnesses the beauty and calm of the morning. His sense of well-being is relaxed and calm. Upon returning home, he takes a stumble and sprains his ankle. Now Rob is feeling upset and frustrated, and he is in pain.

Because of the accident he is running late for work, making him anxious as he needs to attend an important meeting. He calls work to advise that he will be late. Rob's manger tells him not to worry as the meeting was canceled. Now Rob experiences a sense of relief.

Rob arrives at work when he is informed that his boss wants to speak to him; Rob is now worried. Rob meets with his boss, who tells him that he is receiving a promotion. Rob is now feeling excited and very happy. At the end of the day, Rob drives home but winds up in a minor traffic accident. A car rear ends his new vehicle. Rob is now irate.

This scenario illustrates how Rob's state of being is constantly changing; based on the situations and events that he experiences. In the course of one day, Rob went from relaxed, calm, upset, frustrated, anxious, relieved, worried, excited, happy, and irate. There is nothing wrong with experiencing these emotions, our emotions are what make us human. The problem is that our emotions affect our state of well-being, even our identity, that is, how we see ourselves.

Rob's state of well-being, and his sense of identity, was being determined by the situations and events that he encountered. Most of us are like this. We allow the ever-changing circumstances of our lives to determine how we feel about ourselves and the world around us. We are like the person in the movie theater who is totally absorbed with the movie as he experiences a roller coaster ride of thoughts, emotions, and feelings, all dictated by a scene that is being observed at the time.

There is another way to live, one where our state of happiness and well-being is not determined by our situations or circumstances, nor is it affected by our thoughts and emotions. This is the state of life where our sense of well-being is based solely on the wisdom and understanding of who we are, at the deeper level of our being. This is what it means to become enlightened, to understand ourselves at a level that goes beyond experiences and appearances.

When we think of enlightenment, or an enlightened being, we may think of a guru or a wise sage, that enlightenment is reserved for the few and that it takes a great amount of time and practice to achieve it. The truth is, none of these beliefs are true.

You do not have to develop enlightenment, nor do you have to find it. Enlightenment is found within every human being. The potentiality or seed for enlightenment is there within you already. You always had it, and you always will. Even when you pass away, your enlightenment continues on.

The problem is not that you do not have enlightenment, the problem is that you do not realize it.

The reason you do not realize it is because you experience illusions of the mind; you are caught-up in the movie within your mind. The purpose of Buddhism is to see through these illusions so that your enlightenment can be experienced and known by you.

CHAPTER 3
BUDDHIST BELIEFS ON...

God

Buddhism does not believe in a God that is separate from ourselves or outside of ourselves. Many religions, such as Christianity, view God as an omnipotent power that oversees our lives, passes judgments on us and is in charge of our lives.

In general, most Buddhist sects believe in what is best described as an ultimate reality. This ultimate reality is the source which everything arises from, while at the same time it is found within all things. We, and this ultimate reality, are not separate from each other; in fact, we are it. Our lives and ultimate reality are one.

This ultimate reality does not pass judgment; it does not seek our devotion or belief in it. Judgment, punishment, reward, heaven or hell, good or bad, right or wrong, and devotion or disbelief are all created in the mind. When we can understand our minds, we can understand ourselves. When we understand ourselves, we become enlightened. Enlightenment has always existed within us, and it always will. The purpose of Buddhism is to get us to realize this for ourselves through direct experience.

Nirvana

Nirvana is the ultimate liberation for a human being. It comes about through achieving enlightenment and allowing one to transcend his or her karma. All of our sufferings arise from the incorrect perceptions and thoughts that lead us to feeling separate from others and from life itself. Such feelings of separation can lead us to believe we are limited, lacking, flawed, or powerless to change our situations.

The Illusions of the Mind

Our world is full of illusions. To be more accurate, our minds create illusions of the world. These illusions seem so real to us that we rarely question them. When we gaze at a star, we believe that it currently exists; though this is not accurate. The star that we are looking at may have burned out hundreds or even thousands of years ago. Because of its vast distance from Earth, it takes this span of time for its light to travel close enough for us to observe it.

When we view the world around us, we see color.

Grass is green, the sky is blue, there are red sports cars and black cats. However, all these things are actually colorless; they only appear to have a color. Light has various colored wave-lengths; red, yellow, green, and blue. When light shines on an object, those wave lengths that are not absorbed by the object will be reflected off it. A red sports car appears to be red because all the wave lengths are absorbed by the car, except for the red wave-length. The red wave-length is reflected off the car and perceived by our eyes, giving the impression that the car is red.

The planet we live on is both round and continuously orbiting the sun at high speeds, yet we experience the world as flat and motionless.

If you snap your fingers, you may think that the snapping sound and the act of snapping your fingers occur at the same time; however, this is incorrect. Light travels at a faster speed than sound, so the observing of the snapping action is received by the brain before the sound of the snap reaches your ears. The illusion of these things happening simultaneously is the result of the brain making adjustments for the differences when the sensory information is received by you.

A brick seems solid, yet at the atomic level, we know that its true composition is that of energy and sub-atomic particles separated by vast distances of space.

Further, the brain is unable to distinguish between an

imagined object from one that is observed, meaning that your brain cannot tell the difference between a rose that you are observing in a garden from a rose that you are visualizing in your mind.

These are only just a few examples of illusions that we experience on a daily basis. While these examples of illusions may have little consequence for our lives, there are illusions that have a profound impact on our emotional well-being.

Impermanency

One of the most important teachings of the Buddha has to do with impermanency. In fact, the root of humanities suffering is created by it. This illusion is one of the primary causes of war, violence, unhappiness, or a lack of fulfillment. But before we can understand impermanency, we first need to examine the role that the conditioning of our society has on the way we view our world and ourselves.

From the time we are small children, we are conditioned to focus on the world outside of ourselves. An infant knows from its first day that its survival is dependent on its parents. It looks toward its parents for nourishment, comfort, affection, and protection. This continues throughout childhood; the child learns that it needs to appease its parents in order to get their approval. To not appease its parents could result in disapproval and the inability to gain what it desires.

This outward focus expands as we grow older. We focus on school, our teachers, our friends, our employers, our peer group, the media, and our culture. We become very aware of what others are doing, what they think of us, how we fit in, how we can appease them, and how we can gain their favor. All in the attempt to feel good about ourselves, to feel we belong, and to acquire what we feel we need. At the same time, our society does not encourage us to explore our emotions and feelings, to express them, or to get to know ourselves.

In short, our socialization leads to the typical person lacking a sense of self, a sense of self that is free from the expectations, approval, and disapproval of others. Our sense of self-worth is frequently dependent on the conditions that lie outside ourselves, conditions such as the people we know, how much money we make, the work we do, our role in the family, our possessions, our physical appearance, how we dress, the music we listen to, where we live, and so on.

It is this kind of outward focus that leads to most of our sufferings and problems. The reason for this goes to the principle of impermanence, which states all phenomenal aspects of life are an illusion. Anything that we can see, smell, hear, touch, measure, or weigh is considered phenomenal, meaning all of experience is phenomenal.

The world of phenomena is considered an illusion because it is impermanent as it is constantly changing; it cannot be depended on. Relationships come and go, money is gained and lost, our possession will eventually break down; we can lose our jobs; our physical appearance will change with age; our bodies will become feeble, and the people we know will die.

The phenomenal world also exists within us. Our thoughts, our beliefs, our emotions, and our feelings are also in constant flux. We have learned to focus on the outer world to acquire what we desire or need, be it material goods or the approval of others, yet this same world is uncertain and constantly changing.

This dependence on that which cannot be depended upon is the cause of the majority of our problems. Buddhism teaches us how to reveal that aspect of our life which is non-phenomenal; that part of us that never changes, that part of us which is eternal.

Non-substantiality

Another illusion of the mind is revealed through the principle of non-substantiality. The principle of non-substantiality teaches us that there is nothing in this universe that is a complete entity unto itself.

The opposite of non-substantiality is to view life with a sense of separateness, which is the prevailing view of our society. Under this view, you see yourself as a separate and distinct individual from other people; from animals or plants, and from life itself. You see yourself as a person that experiences life, rather than you and life being one.

It is this sense of separateness that we justify discrimination, sexism, prejudice, bigotry, violence, crime, segregation, income inequality, war, imperialism, exploitation, invasions, the destruction of the environment, and the killing of other species.

Within the individual, a sense of separateness can lead to problems as well. Feelings of isolation, loneliness, depression, and many other forms of mental or emotional dysfunctions are due to a sense of not being connected to life.

Buddhism teaches that there is no such thing as a separate self. We can easily understand this by using a rose bush as an example. Most of us would consider a rose bush a distinct entity unto itself. We would view the rosebush as being separate from other rose bushes, separate from the other plants around it, separate from the animals that live around it, and most certainly, separate from us. If asked what the rose bush was made up of, we would most probably mention things such as a stem, leaves, roots, and the rose blossom itself.

Through the Buddhist perspective, we would see the rosebush in a drastically different way. The rosebush is dependent on the soil and the nutrients that it contains. It is also dependent on the rain for its moisture.

Rain comes from clouds, and clouds are formed from the condensation of moisture from the air. This moisture is the result of water from streams, oceans, and lakes evaporating under the heat of the sun. The rosebush also relies on the sun for its ability to create its food through photosynthesis.

The rosebush also depends on the wind, insects, and birds to transfer it seeds and pollen so that it may reproduce. The rosebush also depends on the gardener to trim it, provide it with fertilizer and other forms of care.

We can call all these things; the soil, the rain, the sun, the gardener, etc., as non-rosebush components. Non-rosebush components are not the rosebush, but they make the existence of the rosebush possible. Without even a single non-rosebush component, it would not be possible for the rosebush to even exist.

In short, everything in the universe is a non-rosebush component. The rosebush is not a separate entity unto itself; the rosebush is the conglomerate of everything that exists. The fact that the rosebush exists is evidence that the universe exists. Further, each non-rosebush component is equally a conglomerate of the universe.

Your body is made-up of the universe as well; your body is made of non-human body components. Some of the same elements found in stars are found in your body. Your body fluids have a similar composition to seawater, and your body could not exist if there was no rain, clouds, or the sun. More profoundly, your genes contain genetic material from your parents, your ancestors, and every organism that ever lived. You are not separate from the universe, and you are not just in the universe; you are the universe experienced as physical body.

If we see ourselves separate from the rest of our family, our family will suffer. If we see ourselves separate from our communities, our communities will decline. If our species continues to believe it is separate from the rest of the world, we will destroy ourselves.

In truth, you could not be separate even if you wanted to. Any sense of separation or independence from life is just an illusion; a very costly illusion as evidenced by the state of today's world.

Karma

Karma is a word that has become a lexicon of popular culture; however, it is frequently misunderstood. Karma is the Sanskrit word for 'action,' and it has three components to it: action, memory, and desire. Let us use the example of your favorite food. The first time you ever tasted your favorite food, a chain of events took place.

The first event was desire; you had the desire to taste the food. In order to taste the food, you had to take action; you had to reach out for the food and then taste it. The experience of tasting the food created a memory of the experience. This memory then created a desire to eat more of that food. The same thing can happen with foods you do not like, the difference being is that the memory of the food results in the desire to avoid the food in the future.

We can say that karma are those habitual behaviors, ways of thinking, and ways of feeling, that determine the course of our lives. The challenge is that our karma is so ingrained in us that we are often unaware of it, it becomes subconscious. We mistakenly believe that our karma is simply who we are; it becomes part of our identity. The only difference between Bill Gates and a person who lives a destitute existence is their karma.

In many religions and societies, karma is viewed as being fixed, that it cannot be changed, or that it takes many lifetimes to change; however, this is far from being true. Your karma is being propagated by you, and you only. Let us go back to the example of your favorite food. Every time you eat your favorite food, you have completed a karmic moment. As soon as you have eaten your food, you have completed the karmic cycle; it has ended. You perpetuate your karma the next time you eat your favorite food. If you chose to not eat your favorite food in the future, you would have broken this particular karmic cycle.

Naturally, each one of us has innumerable kinds of karma, and it would take much effort and time to end our bad karma, which is why practicing Buddhism can create a major shift in your life. Instead of tackling each individual karma, Buddhism teaches how to bring out your inherent wisdom, which will automatically cause all of your negative karma to lose their potency. It does this by leading you to a greater level of awareness. That is what it takes to change karma; awareness. Your raised awareness is like the rising sun. The rising sun's light causes the light of the stars to fade. The rising sun is your ever-expanding awareness, while the stars are your negative karma.

Oneness of the Individual and the Environment

Another principle that is similar to non-substantiality is the oneness of the individual and the environment. This principle is based on the interdependence that occurs among all things, which in this case involves the individual being and their environment.

To understand the significance of this principle, all we

need to do is to look at the challenges our world faces today. Most of the problems that humanity faces are the result of not seeing the oneness of our lives with our environment.

War, discrimination, destruction of our natural resources, pollution, the growing decline of biodiversity among animal and plant species, nuclear weapons, and many of our political decisions, reflect a lack of understanding that our action affect our surroundings, and our surroundings affect us.

We, and our environment, are not two separate things; rather, we are directly connected. There are numerous examples of this relationship. A person who is depressed stops cleaning his or her living quarters. As their living quarters become increasingly untidy, it further adds to their sense of unhappiness. A company pollutes the surrounding area with toxic materials, which in turn leads to the people in the area developing cancer and other illnesses. A family has a spouse that engages in disruptive activities such as substance abuse, excessive drinking, having an affair, or gambling. The consequences of these activities then destroys the family unit.

The actions of the individual are a form of karma and karma is not restricted to the individual as karma is shared among people. Nothing that we think, say, or do escapes the detection of the universe. Whatever we do, it will have an effect on our surroundings, and the consequences will return to us.

Ten Worlds

The ten worlds are a model in Buddhist philosophy that depicts the various life states that a person can occupy; these states are hell, hunger, anger, animality, humanity, heaven, learning, realization, bodhisattva, and Buddhahood. These worlds are not outside ourselves; rather, they represent the states of our life force. Hell is the lowest state while Buddhahood is the highest. The following is a description of each of the worlds:

Hell: As previously stated, hell is the lowest life-state a human can occupy. This tenth world is characterized by the feeling that we are the targets of an onslaught of misfortunes from life, and we are powerless to change our situation. This the state of life that leads some people to turn to alcohol or substance abuse, or suicide; they see no hope for a better future.

Hunger: The world of hunger, is the second lowest world and is characterized by someone who has an insatiable need that can never be fulfilled. Whether it is relationships, money, power, or approval, this person is relentless in their pursuit of that which they hunger for.

This hunger is just an illusion, for if they manage to obtain that which they want, they will be satisfied only momentarily. This person will experience a brief period of satisfaction before experiencing a need to satisfy another desire. Examples of this would be people who are addicted to relationships, alcohol, drugs, power, prestige, or attention.

Animality: Animality is the third lowest world, and is characterized by the state of life where a person exhibits animal-like qualities in the way they relate with other people. They dominate or intimidate those that they see as being weaker than themselves but try to appease those that they view as being more powerful. The world of animality can be considered the Law of the Jungle. Examples of this world can be found everywhere from the schoolyard bully to Wall Street.

Anger: Anger is the fourth lowest state, and manifests in a person as the need to dominate or win over others. Because this intention is concealed by the way the person conducts themselves, it is considered a higher world than animality.

Humanity: The world of humanity, is the fifth lowest world and is characterized by the state of life where the person does not feel a real sense of suffering or need but at the same time the person is vulnerable to having their sense of identity or autonomy defined by external factors, such as changing situations and events.

Heaven: This is the sixth lowest world, and is characterized by experiences of elation, real joy, and other enjoyable emotions that are associated with achieving a desired goal. The challenge for the world of Heaven is that these experiences are fleeting. The positive aspects of the world of Heaven are not stable.

The previous six worlds are referred to as the lower worlds as they allow us to be heavily influenced by our surroundings; we become stimulus-response beings, whose sense of self is shaped largely by our experiences of life. The next four worlds are referred to as the higher worlds.

Learning: The seventh world, the world of learning, involves developing a greater sense of openness in our lives, to deeper understanding and wisdom. This is why music, art, and poetry can be so powerful. They can resonate with us and lead us to developing a deeper insight about ourselves. This is also the role of religion or spirituality, to get us to stop focusing so much on the physical world and more on our inner world.

Realization: The world of realization, is the eighth world and is similar to the world of learning, with one exception. Instead of relying on sources of inspiration outside ourselves to get in touch with ourselves, we develop a depth of awareness in which the truths of our lives become self-evident.

Bodhisattva: The ninth world, the world of the Bodhisattva, is when we dedicate our life to discovering the truth of who we are, to become enlightened. But this dedication to seeking enlightenment must be connected with working toward the happiness of others. It is through working for the happiness of others that makes room for the emergence of our enlightened nature.

The last three worlds are considered the higher worlds because they become increasingly less influenced by our environment. Rather than reacting, we increasingly respond to life with wisdom, compassion, and courage. Rather than basing our sense of self on the world outside ourselves, our sense of being is increasingly anchored in our enlightened nature, also known as the Buddha nature.

Buddhahood: The tenth world, is that of Buddhahood. This is a world that is very difficult to explain in words as it exists beyond our conceptual understanding. The world of Buddha can be best described through the qualities of ultimate freedom, unceasing equanimity, and boundless wisdom. In the world of Buddhahood, all sense of separateness, limitation, and suffering dissolve, for Buddhahood is pure consciousness.

Most of us enter the world of Buddhahood on a regular basis; we inhabit the tenth and highest world whenever we go into deep sleep. In deep sleep, all sense of individuality, personality, identity, and separation cease to exist, as does thoughts. Without thoughts, there is no experience in deep sleep; we escape the illusions of the mind and enter pure consciousness.

The Ten Worlds are mutually inclusive of each other, meaning that each world contains the remaining nine worlds within it. This means that regardless of which of the nine worlds we are in, the world of Buddhahood lies within us. It also means that the world of Buddhahood has the other nine worlds in it, including the lowest world, Hell.

Throughout the day, we typically shift from world to world, though each of us has a baseline world, the world we spend most of our time in. When we are in the world of Buddhahood, all the lower worlds function in a manner that supports us in our happiness. These lower worlds exhibit their noble qualities so as to enhance our lives. Without the wisdom of enlightenment, the lower worlds experience their illusionary state, which leads to suffering.

The Four Noble Truths

The Four Noble Truths are a foundational Buddhist principle from which many Buddhist teachings are based on. The Four Noble Truths are as follows:

The first Noble Truth is regarding suffering, which is also known as *Dukkha*. Dukkha is the term used for all sufferings, from the very mild to the most severe. Suffering is an inescapable aspect of living in this world, this is the first Noble Truth.

The second Noble Truth is that Dukkha is causal in its appearance in this world. The cause of Dukkha comes from our tendency toward attachments or aversion. Any time we try to control life by grasping or clinging to the physical world, it will lead to suffering. Similarly, when holding an aversion toward anything in life, this too will lead to suffering. All of this is based on the impermanence of life. The suffering arises because we identify with that which we are attached to, or that we are avoiding.

The third Noble Truth is cessation of Dukkha, which is called *Nirvana*. Nirvana arises when we no longer identify with the world of form, including our bodies and thoughts. Nirvana can also be referred to as the Tenth World, the world of Buddhahood.

The Fourth Noble Truth is also referred to as the *Eight Fold Path*; these are the eight paths that lead to Awakening.

The first path, is the path of the correct view or understanding, meaning that we are able to perceive the illusions of the mind. The Sanskrit word for this path is

Samma-Ditthi.

The second path, is the path of correct thought. Correct thought comes from viewing the world through love and compassion. This path is known as *Samma-Sankappa*. Love and compassion arises when we are able to understand our own suffering and are not ruled by our attachments.

The third path, is the path of correct speech. Correct speech is that which is compassionate, heartfelt, honest, inspiring, and understood by the listener.

The fourth path, is the path of correct action, which is action that creates value for all stakeholders; it is ethical, and upholds our sense of dignity. This path is referred to as *Samma-Kammanta.*

The fifth path, is the path of correct livelihood. This means that how we generate an income for ourselves is ethical and does not lead to exploitation of others. This is known as *Samma-Ajiva.*

The sixth path, is the path of correct effort or energy. This can be understood as focus and diligence. This occurs when we are consciously focusing our life force for the purpose of transforming or creating value, or benefit for others and ourselves; we become conscious creators who are taking action that is in alignment with all of life. The sixth path is known as *Samma-Vayama.*

The seventh path, is that of mindfulness. Mindfulness

is an expanded awareness to all levels of experience. It means having awareness of our environment, other people, our thoughts, feelings, perceptions, and the nature of reality itself. This awareness is not a conceptual understanding; it is a deeper knowing that comes when we can experience our world in a way that is free of the illusions created by our minds. The seventh path is known as *Samma-Sati*.

The eighth path is difficult to describe in words but it involves becoming fully integrated, becoming one with our experience. It involves meditating so deeply that all sense of distinction or separateness fades and we become one with all. This is the meaning of Buddhahood or enlightenment. This final path is known as *Samma-Samadhi*.

The Middle Way

The Middle Way is a familiar term to most of us; however, its meaning is often misunderstood. The Middle Way refers to understanding reality at a deeper level than our conditioned minds will allow. Our minds have been conditioned by society, our culture, our education, and our up-bringing, to perceive the world in a dualistic manner, as described earlier in this book.

An example of the Middle Way would be the mind-body connection. From one perspective, the mind and body appear to be separate from each other. The body is evident to us as we can see and touch it. The mind is not as evident. No one has ever seen a mind, nor can we touch it; the mind lacks any physical quality to it, having no shape, color, or size to it. For these reasons, believing that the mind and body are separate is understandable. This separation is an example of duality.

But the belief that the mind and body are one is also a reasonable assertion. It is proven that the mind affects the functioning of the body and body affects the mind. The Middle Way recognizes this paradox, seeing the truth in both sides of the argument.

When we can understand the paradox of separateness and unity in all phenomena, we avoid the traps of our thinking that prevents us from experiencing a deeper level of reality. The Middle Way is not some lofty philosophy or abstract idea, it is both very practical and necessary. It is practical because by questioning societal beliefs, and looking more deeply, we have an opportunity to address the problems of society, which were largely caused by not realizing the interdependence and connection that is found in all of life.

We create problems in our world, both individually and collectively, when we see ourselves as being separate from the rest of life, when we fail to see that anything we do has a ripple effect that travels the expanse of the universe.

CHAPTER 4
LIVING BUDDHIST TEACHINGS

AFTER READING THE previous chapters in this book, you may conclude that Buddhist teachings are too difficult to understand or practice, that it would require a lot of work, or you may be concerned that practicing these teachings may conflict with your religious beliefs.

My hope is that you will not let any of these concerns discourage you. First of all, though Buddhism is recognized as a religion that was not its original intent. Buddhism is more of a science of the mind. It views the world in a practical and realistic manner that is testable; it does not require faith. More important than faith is your actual experience when practicing its teachings. If you find that its teachings enrich your life, then faith will follow.

Buddhist teachings are applicable to any religious or spiritual tradition that you may belong to, even science is reaching conclusions that mirror Buddhist thought. For this reason, you do not have to give-up your religious beliefs; you do not even have to consider yourself Buddhist.

This book is in no way intended to teach you how to

become a Buddhist. If this is your desire, I recommend you contact a Buddhist community within your neighborhood. But if you want to apply some if its principles and philosophies in your life, the following are suggestions on how to do so:

God

There many beliefs about God; however, often these beliefs are cultivated through our upbringing and are never challenged or explored by us. One of the most primary questions we can ask ourselves about our beliefs or disbeliefs of God, is my belief about God just that, a belief?

A belief is simply a thought that we give a lot of attention to; our attention to a thought makes it true for us. We can only experience that which the conceptual mind understands, meaning that we if we cannot detect something, we cannot have an experience of it. What about our sense of self that which we call 'I.' Can this be detected? Where is this 'I' located? Is it located in the 'body?' Is it located in the heart or mind? Regardless of how you answer these questions, you would then have to ask, who knows this? Who is aware of you? How can we claim to know God without first understanding the true nature of who we are?

Here are some practical steps you can take to explore the

nature of yourself:

1. Regardless of what you believe about God or yourself, take time daily to become quiet and still. You can meditate or simply find a relaxing place to sit and become still within, do not judge, evaluate, analyze, or think about anything, just observe.

2. Observe your thoughts, your sensations, your emotions, your feelings, the people around you, or your environment. Do not put any effort in your observation, just allow your attention to roam freely.

3. The only thing you need to do is observe. Allow whatever happens to happen on its own accord. By practicing this exercise, you will learn to observe more deeply as you will have reduced the influence of the mind. With that will come a clearer understanding to the nature of God and you.

The Illusions of the Mind

1. Close your eyes and imagine a black cat in your mind, make the image as vivid as possible.

2. Now imagine a fireplace, again make it as vivid as possible.

3. Lastly, imagine a full moon, make it as real as you can.

4. Now open your eyes. The back cat, the fireplace, and the full moon were simply thoughts you held in your mind; however, at no point did you believe that you were any of these objects.

5. If you do not believe you are these thoughts, then why are you so convinced of the beliefs that you have of yourself, other people, or life itself?

6. The only difference between a random thought and a deeply held conviction is the amount of attention we give it.

Impermanency

1. Take some time to be calm. Now observe something. It can be anything; an object, a person, your own body, or nature.

2. As you observe your subject, ask yourself is there anything about this object that is not impermanent? That is not subject to change?

3. If your answer is yes, then look more deeply. Nothing that we can experience through our thoughts or five senses is free from change.

Non-substantiality

1. Take time to calm down your mind and then observe an object.

2. Take time to reflect on all the things that are required for this object to exist.

3. As you come up with a list of such things, consider what these things depend upon for their existence.

4. Ask yourself, what if any of these things did not exist, could this object exist?

5. Consider the object again. Is this object truly an independent existence, or is an expression of all the things it depends on?

Karma

Karma is our habitual ways of thinking or behaving, which has become ingrained in us. For this reason, we often do not notice our Karma, or if we do, we feel there is not much we can do about it. The key to changing karma is awareness.

1. Start becoming more aware of your daily thinking and actions.

2. When you catch yourself thinking a habitual thought or behaving in a habitual way, ask yourself the following questions:

   a. Do I have a choice of thinking or behaving differently?

   b. Is there a payoff for me thinking or behaving in this habitual way?

   c. How would I like to think as opposed to my current habitual thinking?

   d. How would I like to behave as opposed to my current habitual behavior?

   e. Would these new ways of thinking or behaving retain the payoff that my current thinking or behaving offers?

   f. Would these new ways of thinking or behaving bring me greater happiness?

3. If you said yes to the last two questions, start incorporating your new way of thinking or behaving in your daily life.

4. Whenever you catch yourself repeating your old thinking or behavior, remind yourself that you are now dedicated to your new ways of being.

Oneness of the individual and the environment

1. As in the previous practices, start off with a sense of calmness in your mind.

2. Now reflect on all the ways that you affect the people around you, the physical environment around you, or the natural environment around you. Do not limit your reflection to your locality, consider the entire planet and your physical body as well. Your physical body is the environment for

your inner world of thoughts, emotions, feelings, and perceptions.

3. When you have finished reflecting on your effect on your environment, reflect how your local and global environment affect you.

4. When you have completed your reflection, ask yourself am I and my environment one, or am I separate from it?

Ten Worlds

1. Review the section on the Ten Worlds and become familiar with them.

2. Throughout the day, take a moment and observe your emotions and state of being.

3. Ask yourself which of the Ten Worlds do I spend most of my time in?

4. Which of the Ten Worlds do I normally experience during the course of the day?

5. This kind of introspection will allow you to understand your current state of life. You can then ask yourself which worlds you would like to experience more often.

6. When you have decided on the world you would like to frequent more often, ask yourself what would you need to believe to make that possible?

7. Condition your thinking to adopt this belief by focusing on all the positive outcomes you would receive by making this new belief your reality. Conversely, think of all the negatives you would experience if you do not change your existing belief.

8. Whenever you find yourself experiencing your new belief, find a way to reward yourself in that moment, even if it is simply telling yourself 'Good job!' You can follow-up later by rewarding yourself in a manner that you find more meaningful.

The Four Noble Truths

Review the section on the Four Noble Truths, remembering that they point to suffering that is caused by incorrect understanding of reality. This incorrect understanding of reality includes the illusions of the mind, attachment, incorrect speech, incorrect action, incorrect livelihood, incorrect effort or expenditure of energy, and a lack of mindfulness.

We can simplify this by reducing these down to one word, 'Love.' I want you to make it a daily goal to come from the point of love in how you perceive, how you think, how you speak, how you act, how you work, and how you expend effort. The following are examples on how to do this:

Perception and the illusions of our mind:
We fall for the illusions of our mind, of our thoughts, because we believe them to be true. Given that many of our thoughts create a sense of fear or concern in us, fear is what is brought into existence, it shows up in our experience.

Turn the tables on your mind and see yourself as the parent and your thoughts and emotions are your children. When you experience thoughts and emotions that create fear in you, view them with a sense of love and appreciation. Do not challenge your thoughts or emotions, do not try to change them, just accept them for what they are and observe them with a sense of love and caring. You can speak to them just as you would speak to a frightened child.

Speaking: Whenever you speak to others or yourself, come from the perspective of love. This means that you do not judge, criticize, or devalue them in any way. Allow your speech to communicate compassion, honesty, and encouragement. Speak to others and yourself in a way that acknowledges that who they are, or who you are, is much greater than what is currently being experienced.

Actions: See your actions not as an end to themselves but rather a way to express who you are in a physical manner. Anybody can take action on a task. Become greater than your past by infusing your actions with a sense of love and compassion for all those who are affected by it.

Livelihood: Demonstrating love through your livelihood can take a variety of forms. It could mean finding a new way to support yourself that is more aligned with your values or it could be performing your current job in a way that causes you to focus on creating value for your employer, for your co-workers, and your customers. When this becomes your focus, you will transcend your job by making your work and expression of your love.

Expenditure of effort and energy: On a daily basis, are you largely directing your effort and energy toward activities in order to meet the expectations of others, or out of a sense of obligation? Or do you direct your energy toward activities that are meaningful for you, that are fulfilling, or out of a desire to create happiness for others and yourself? This has less to do with the nature of the activity than it does the meaning the activity has for you and the value it creates for others.

Make it a goal that you will reserve as much of your efforts and energy for those things that bring you fulfilment. Nature is a master in energy efficiency as all actions that are displayed in the natural world lead to birth and growth, even in death.

When we allow our minds to direct us, much of our energy is spent on engaging in activities out of a sense of fear, guilt, concern for the opinion of others, or distracting ourselves form our thoughts and emotions.

You can select one of these five categories to practice each day of the week, or you can select one category to practice for the whole week. When you practice, commit to taking 3 - 5 minutes to devote to your selected category. As you become more skillful, you can extend this time frame. With continued practice, mindfulness will spontaneously arise within you.

The Middle Way

To practice the Middle Way, commit a few minutes observing the world around you without actively involving thought. For these few minutes, become a blank slate. Forget about your education, what you know, past experience, or any form of judgment. Just observe the world, allowing it the freedom to fully express itself without any interpretations by you. When you can view life free of conceptual thinking, you will experience life in a new way

CONCLUSION

OUR WORLD IS full of challenges, which may seem too complex or difficult to change. We may believe that the needed change must come from our leaders, our government, or others who hold power. The ordinary citizen may believe that there is nothing he or she can do, that the resistance to change that is posed by those in power is unsurmountable.

This belief is what creates a sense of apathy or helplessness and is just another illusion created by the mind. Change starts within the individual. When the individual changes, he or she affects others, causing a domino effect. By challenging our minds and perceptions, each of us can become a change agent. This is the purpose of Buddhism; to create a world that respects the dignity of all lives.

Made in the USA
Columbia, SC
02 July 2019